Contents

Gathering Information

Look at the clothes you are wearing.

What colour are they? Is there a pattern or a picture on them?

This girl's skirt has a colourful plaid pattern.

You are
seeing what
your clothes
look like.

6

Seeing is one of your five senses. You use your eyes to see things.

Eyes help you see to read, colour pictures, do homework and play.

Your sense of sight helps you learn about the world. It can also protect you from danger.

Thanks to your sense of sight, you can take in information and explore your surroundings.

8

Your Eyes

How do your eyes help you see? When you see something, your eyes let in light through the pupils. The pupils are the dark circles in the centre of your eyes.

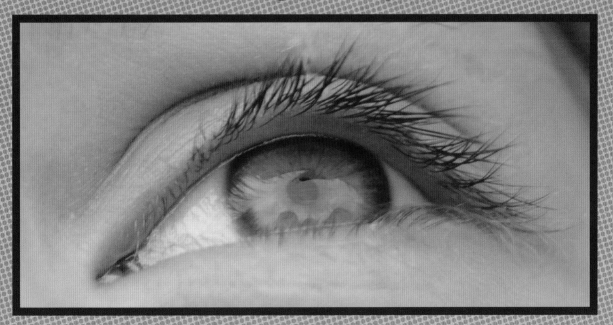

Then the light moves through the curved part of your eyes called the lens.

The lens turns the light into
a picture on the back of your
eyes. The picture is upside
down. But your brain flips the
picture over.

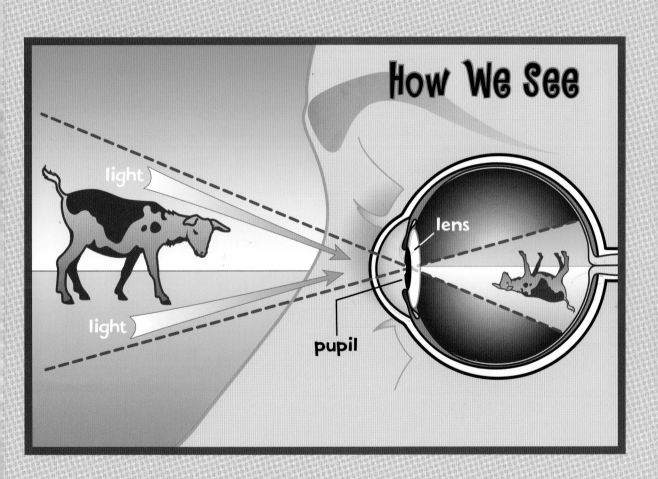

Your eyes help you see both this boy and his reflection in the car window.

Then your brain tells you what you are seeing!

Colours

Your eyes let you see many different colours.

How many colours do you see in this painting?

You can see a green frog.

You can see an orange ice lolly.

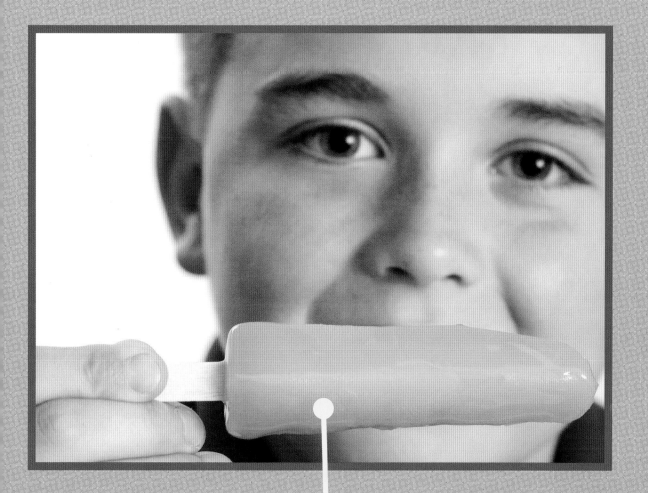

The world is full of beautiful colours – and your eyes let you see them all.

15

Your eyes need light to see different colours.

Without light, you couldn't see these colourful sweets.

It is hard to tell what colour your socks are in the dark!

17

Protection from Danger

Seeing can protect you from danger. You can see when it is safe to cross the street.

Reading signs and watching traffic keep you safe.

19

You can see the exit sign to lead the way out in an emergency.

Distance

Your eyes can see things at different distances.

They can see words in a book that you are holding.

You need good close-up vision to read.

They can see leaves on a tree in your neighbour's garden.

You need good long – distance vision to see trees that are far away.

Some people have trouble seeing things that are far away. They look blurry.

If you are short-sighted then far-away objects - like this sign - can look blurry.

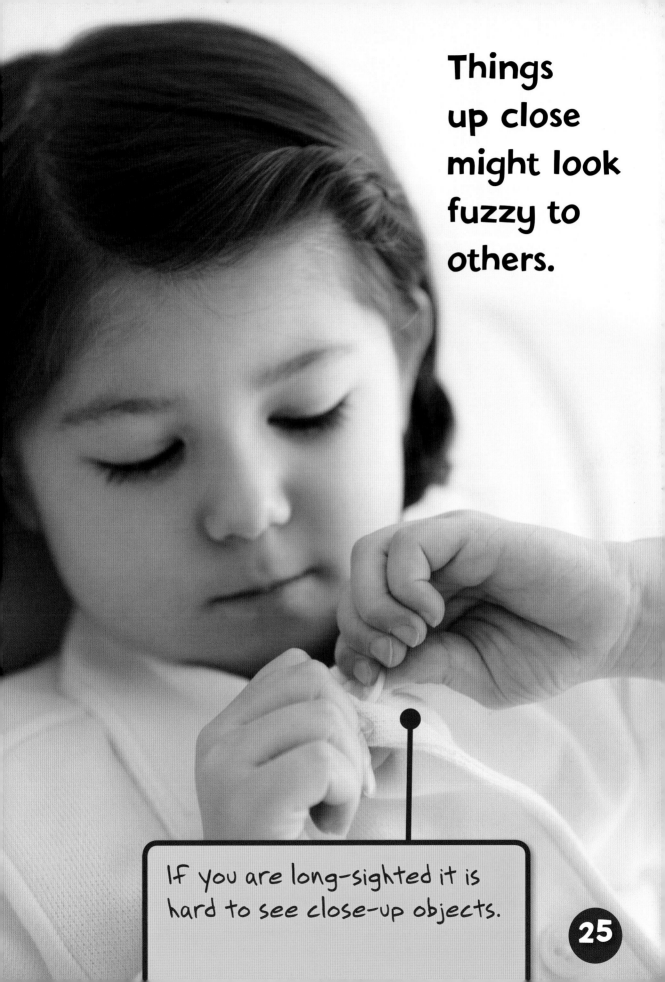

Things up close might look fuzzy to others.

If you are long-sighted it is hard to see close-up objects.

Glasses can
help people
who have
trouble
seeing.
Glasses help
the eyes
focus.

Seeing is an important sense. You use it every day.

This boy is using his sense of sight —as well as his sense of touch — as he plays in a stream.

Activity
Test Your Depth Perception

Depth perception is the ability to judge how far away objects are from one another. Your eyes must work together for you to have good depth perception. Want to see how depth perception works? Ask an adult if you can try this experiment to test your depth perception.

What you need:
Two cotton buds

What you do:

Hold a cotton bud horizontally in each hand. Hold your arms straight out in front of you. Close one eye. (If you can't hold one eye closed, you can ask a friend to gently hold his or her hand over your eye.) Slowly move your hands towards each other and try to touch the ends of the cotton buds together. If you miss, keep trying. Then open both eyes and try again.

It is easier to touch the cotton buds together when you use both of your eyes. That's because your eyes work together to let you see the cotton buds from different angles. Your brain uses the information that it gets from your eyes to help you judge the distance between the cotton buds.

Glossary

blurry: unclear or hard to see

depth perception: the ability to judge how far away objects are from one another

glasses: glass or plastic lenses set in frames. People wear glasses to help their eyes focus.

lens: the curved part of your eye that lets you focus

pupil: the dark circle in the centre of your eye. Your eye lets in light through its pupil.

sense: one of the powers that people and animals use to learn about their surroundings. The five senses are sight, hearing, touch, taste and smell.

Further Reading

Haddon, Jean. *Make Sense!* Minneapolis: Millbrook Press, 2007.

Hewitt, Sally. *Look Here!* New York: Crabtree Publishing Company, 2008.

Kids Health: How the Body Works
http://kidshealth.org/kid/htbw

Nelson, Robin. *Seeing and Hearing Well.* London: Lerner Books, 2008.

Suhr, Mandy. *Sight.* London: Wayland, 2007.

Index

Photo Acknowledgments

The images in this book are used with the permission of: © Tatiana Popova/istockphoto.com, p. 1; © Scott Barrow, Inc./SuperStock, p. 2; © Chris Ladd/Taxi/Getty Images, p. 4; © Julie Caruso/Independent Picture Service, p. 5; © Jamie Grill/Iconica/Getty Images, p. 6; © Gallo Images-Anthony Strack/Gallo images ROOTS RF collection/Getty Images, pp. 7, 22; © Stephan K. Hall/SuperStock, p. 8; © Julie Caruso, p. 9; © Juan Silva/Stone/Getty Images, p. 10; © Laura Westlund/Independent Picture Service, p. 11; © Kohei Hara/Getty Images, p. 12; © age fotostock/SuperStock, p. 13; © Digital Vision/Getty Images, p. 14; © iStockphoto.com/Fertnig, p. 15; © Icefields/Dreamstime.com, p. 16; © David Roth/ Photodisc/Getty Images, p. 17; © Paul Doyle/Alamy, p. 18; © Ian Miles-Flashpoint Pictures/ Alamy, p. 19; © Todd Strand/Independent Picture Service, pp. 20, 24; © David Deas/DK Stock/Getty Images, p. 21; © Gary John Norman/The Image Bank/Getty Images, p. 23; © BLOOMimage/Getty Images, p. 25; © Peter Dazeley/Photographer's Choice RR/Getty Images, p. 26; © iStockphoto.com/asiseeit, p. 27; © iStockphoto.com/StuartDuncanSmith, p. 28; © Kohei Hara/Digital Vision/Getty Images, p. 30; © Zeid/eStock Photo/Alamy, p. 31.

Front cover: © Dwight Eschliman/Stone/Getty Images.

First published in the United States of America in 2010